MW01054358

Looking for a fast and fun quilting project?
Our wonderfully cozy lap quilts and throws with
ragged, exposed seams are just what you've been
waiting for! They're a cinch to make using our
easy techniques for frayed-edge patchwork
and simple machine appliqué.

Just cut, sew and quilt one section at a
time and clip the exposed seams as you go.
Then machine wash your finished quilt and tumble
it dry to create the soft, fluffy three-dimensional
texture. The more you wash, the softer
the seams become.

LEISURE ARTS, INC
Little Rock, AR

Apple Cinnamon

Finished Block Size: 12" x 12" (30 cm x 30 cm)
Finished Size: 65" x 85" (165 cm x 216 cm)

YARDAGE REQUIREMENTS

Yardage is based on 45" (114 cm) wide fabric. Yardage amounts are based on using the same fabrics for the front and back of your quilt.

Quilt:
5/8 yd (57 cm) **each** of 10 assorted prints (blocks)
2 1/4 yds (2.06 m) of cream print (appliqué backgrounds)
1 3/8 yds (1.26 m) of red print (inner border)
1 1/8 yds (1.03 m) **each** of 2 brown prints (outer border)

Appliqué:
1/3 yd (30 cm) of red print (flowers)
1/4 yd (23 cm) of brown print (flower centers)
3/4 yd (69 cm) of green print #1 (leaves and vine)
1/8 yd (11 cm) of green print #2 (leaves)

Other fabrics and notions:
1/2 yd (46 cm) of dark brown print (binding)
6 yds (5.49 m) of osnaburg (used in place of batting)
12 buttons – 3/4" (19 mm) diameter
Sulky KK 2000® Temporary Spray Adhesive
3/8" (9.5 mm) bias pressing bar
Transparent monofilament thread

Before beginning, please read General Instructions, pages 31-35, to familiarize yourself with the techniques used in making this quilt. Use Stitch-and-Clip Method for all seams, unless otherwise noted.

CUTTING

From assorted prints:
- Cut a total of 36 Square A's 9" x 9". (Cut an even number of pieces from each print so that you will have matching pieces for front and back of quilt.)
- Cut a total of 36 Square B's 5" x 5". (Cut an even number of squares from each print.)
- Cut a total of 72 Rectangle C's 5" x 9". (Cut an even number of rectangles from each print.)

From cream print:
- Cut 8 strips 9"w for appliqué backgrounds.

From red print:
- Cut 14 strips 3"w for inner border.

From **each** brown print:
- Cut 7 strips 5"w for outer border.

From osnaburg:
- Cut 10 strips 9"w. From these strips, cut 18 Square A fillers 9" x 9" and 36 Rectangle C fillers 5" x 9".
- Cut 3 strips 5"w. From these strips, cut 18 Square B fillers 5" x 5".
- Cut 4 appliqué background filler strips 9"w.
- Cut 7 inner border filler strips 3"w.
- Cut 7 outer border filler strips 5"w.

MAKING THE APPLIQUÉD BACKGROUNDS

1. For appliqué backgrounds, match **right sides** and use a $1/4$" **seam allowance** to sew 2 cream print strips together end to end to make 1 long strip. Repeat for remaining cream print strips and matching osnaburg strips to make a total of 4 long cream print strips and 2 osnaburg strips.
2. Using spray adhesive to secure, layer 1 print strip (right side down), 1 osnaburg strip, and another cream print strip (right side up) to make 1 long layered strip. Make 2 layered strips.
3. Quilt each Appliqué Background using an allover meandering pattern. Trim each Appliqué Background to 73" long.
4. For vine appliqués, cut a 15" x 15" square from green print #1. Cut $1^1/4$"w bias strips from square. Matching **right sides**, use a $1/4$" **seam allowance** to sew bias strips together end to end to make 2 strips at least 80" long.
5. For each strip, match **wrong** sides and long edges and use a $1/4$" **seam allowance** to sew edges together to form a tube. Trim seam allowance to $1/8$". Centering seam on back of strip, use pressing bar and a hot iron to press each tube flat to complete each vine.
6. Use patterns, page 7, to cut out appliqués.
7. Referring to **Quilt Diagram**, page 6, arrange vines and appliqués on each Appliqué Background. Using spray adhesive to secure, arrange vines and appliqués on each Appliqué Background. Stitch all pieces in place using monofilament thread and a small zigzag stitch to complete each Appliqué Background.

MAKING THE BLOCKS

1. Using spray adhesive to secure, layer 1 Square A (right side down), 1 matching filler, and another matching Square A (right side up). Repeat to make 18 Square A's, 18 Square B's, and 36 Rectangle C's.

2. Place 1 layered Square A and 1 layered Rectangle C back sides together. Sew along 1 long edge using $1/2$" seam allowance. Clip seam at $1/2$" intervals up to, but not through, the stitching line. Open and lay flat to make Unit 1. Make 18 Unit 1's.

Unit 1 (make 18)

3. Sew 1 layered Square B and 1 layered Rectangle C along 1 short edge to make Unit 2. Make 18 Unit 2's.

Unit 2 (make 18)

4. Sew 1 Unit 1 and 1 Unit 2 together to make Block. Make 18 Blocks.

Block (make 18)

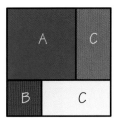

5. Machine quilt each Block, using a meandering pattern. When quilting, move around seams on the outside edge or through clipped seams to quilt entire Block.

ASSEMBLING THE QUILT

*Refer to **Quilt Diagram** to assemble quilt.*

1. Arrange 6 blocks into a row, turning blocks as desired so that colors are contrasting. Sew blocks together to form Row. Make 3 Rows.
2. Sew Rows and Appliqué Backgrounds together to form Quilt Center.
3. For inner border, match **right sides** and use a ¼" **seam allowance** to sew 7 inner border strips together end to end to make 1 long strip; do not clip seam allowances. Repeat for remaining inner border and inner border filler strips. Follow Step 2 of **Making The Appliquéd Backgrounds**, page 5, to layer inner border strips.
4. Machine quilt layered strip using meandering pattern.
5. From each quilted strip, cut two 57" long Top/Bottom Inner Borders and two 73" long Side Inner Borders.
6. Sew Side, then Top and Bottom Inner Borders to Quilt Center.
7. For outer border, alternate fabrics and sew 7 outer border strips together in same manner as inner border. Repeat for remaining outer border and outer border filler strips. Layer strips in same manner as inner border.
8. Machine quilt layered strips using meandering pattern.
9. From quilted strip, cut two 65" long Top/Bottom Outer Borders and two 77" long Side Outer Borders.
10. Sew Side, then Top and Bottom Outer Borders to Inner Border.
11. Sew 1 button to each flower center.
12. Follow **Binding**, page 34, to bind quilt.
13. Follow **Washing**, page 35, to wash and fluff quilt seams.

Quilt Diagram

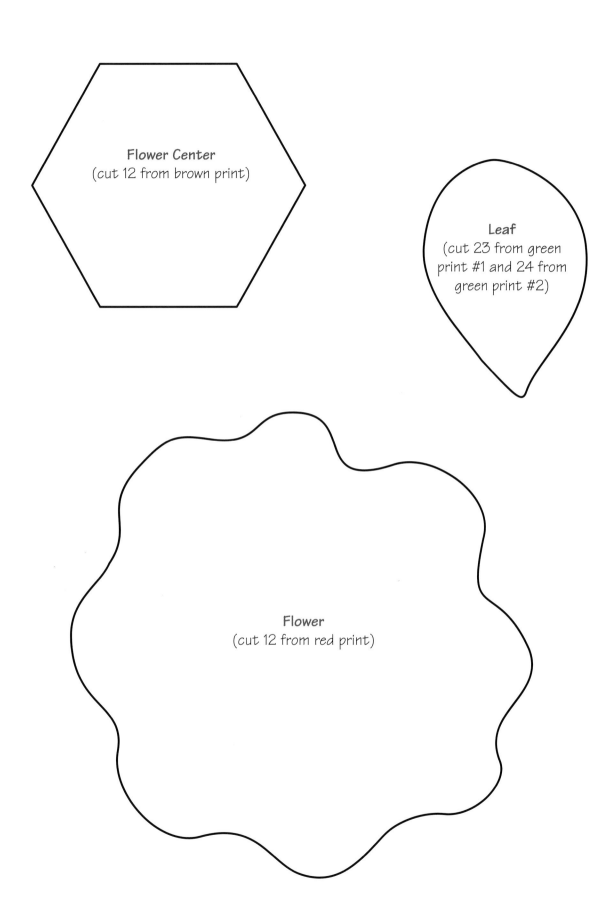

Flower Center
(cut 12 from brown print)

Leaf
(cut 23 from green print #1 and 24 from green print #2)

Flower
(cut 12 from red print)

Juliann

Finished Block Size: 11" x 11" (28 cm x 28 cm)
Finished Size: 58½" x 71½" (149 cm x 182 cm)

YARDAGE REQUIREMENTS

Yardage is based on 45" (114 cm) wide fabric. Yardage amounts are based on using the same fabrics for the front and back of your quilt.

Quilt:
 ½ yd (46 cm) **each** of 8 assorted cream prints (appliqué backgrounds)
 2⅛ yds (1.94 m) of light green print (sashing)
 2⅝ yds (2.4 m) of medium green print (outer border)
 1 yd (91 cm) of dark green print (inner border)

Appliqué:
 6 fat quarters of assorted peach prints (flowers)
 ½ yd (46 cm) of burgundy print (flower centers)

Other fabrics:
 ¾ yd (69 cm) of burgundy print (binding)
 4⅜ yds (4.0 m) of osnaburg (used in place of batting)
 48 buttons – ½" (13 mm) diameter
 Sulky KK 2000® Temporary Spray Adhesive
 Transparent monofilament thread (optional)

Before beginning, please read General Instructions, pages 31-35, to familiarize yourself with the techniques used in making this quilt. Use Stitch-and-Clip Method for all seams, unless otherwise noted.

CUTTING

From assorted cream prints:
 • Cut a total of 24 Appliqué Backgrounds 13" x 13". (Cut an even number of pieces from each print so that you will have matching pieces for front and back of quilt.)

From light green print:
 • Cut 22 strips 3"w for sashing.

From medium green print:
 • Cut 12 strips 7"w for outer border.

From dark green print:
 • Cut 10 strips 3"w for inner border.

From osnaburg:
 • Cut 4 strips 13"w. From these strips, cut 12 appliqué background fillers 13" x 13".
 • Cut 16 strips 3"w. Use 11 strips for sashing fillers and 5 strips for inner border fillers.
 • Cut 6 outer border filler strips 7"w.

MAKING THE BLOCKS

1. Using spray adhesive to secure, layer 1 appliqué background (face down), 1 appliqué background filler, and another appliqué background (face up). Repeat to make 12 Appliqué Backgrounds.

2. Use patterns, page 13, to cut out appliqués. Using spray adhesive and making sure to center pieces carefully, arrange appliqués on each Appliqué Background. Stitch in place using monofilament thread and a small zigzag stitch or coordinating thread and machine buttonhole stitch to complete each Appliqué Unit.

Appliqué Unit (make 12)

3. Cut each Appliqué Unit in 4 equal parts (**Fig. 1**) to make a total of 48 Quarter-Block Units.

Fig. 1

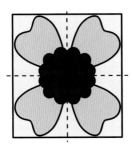

Quarter-Block Units (make 48)

4. For 1 Block, select 4 different Quarter-Block Units. Place 2 of the units back sides together. Sew along 1 edge using ¹/₂" seam allowance. Clip seam at ¹/₂" intervals up to, but not through, the stitching line. Open and lay flat to make Half-Block Unit.

Half-Block Unit

5. Repeat with remaining 2 blocks to make another Half-Block Unit.

Half-Block Unit

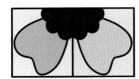

6. Sew units together, making sure to clip afterwards, to complete Block. Repeat to make a total of 12 Blocks.

Block (make 12)

ASSEMBLING THE QUILT

1. For inner sashing, use spray adhesive to layer 1 light green strip (face down), 1 osnaburg strip, and another light green strip (face up). Repeat to make a total of 11 layered strips.
2. Machine quilt each strip as shown, using quilting pattern, page 13, and repeating as needed.

Inner Sashing Strip

3. From quilted strips, cut 5 Long Sashings 3" x 41" and 16 Short Sashings 3" x 12".
4. Sew 4 Short Sashings and 3 Blocks together to make Row. Make 4 Rows.

Row (make 4)

5. Sew Long Sashings and Rows together to make Quilt Center.

6. For inner border, match **right sides** and use a **¹/₄" seam allowance** to sew 5 inner border strips together end to end to make 1 long strip; do not clip seam allowances. Repeat for remaining inner border strips and inner border filler strips. Follow Step 1 to layer inner border strips.

7. Machine quilt layered strip using same pattern as used on sashing.

8. From quilted strip, cut two 59" long Side Inner Borders and two 42" long Top/Bottom Inner Borders.

9. Sew Top, Bottom, then Side Inner Borders to Quilt Center.

10. For outer border, sew 6 outer border strips together in same manner as inner border. Repeat for remaining outer border and outer border filler strips. Layer strips in same manner as inner border.

11. Machine quilt outer border using a meandering pattern.

12. Cut two 71" long Side Outer Borders and two 46" long Top/Bottom Outer Borders.

13. Sew Top, Bottom, then Side Outer Borders to Inner Border.

14. Sew 4 buttons to each flower center.

15. Follow **Binding**, page 34, to bind quilt using a 3¹/₂"w bias strip and a ¹/₂" seam allowance.

16. Follow **Washing**, page 35, to wash quilt to fluff seams.

Quilt Diagram

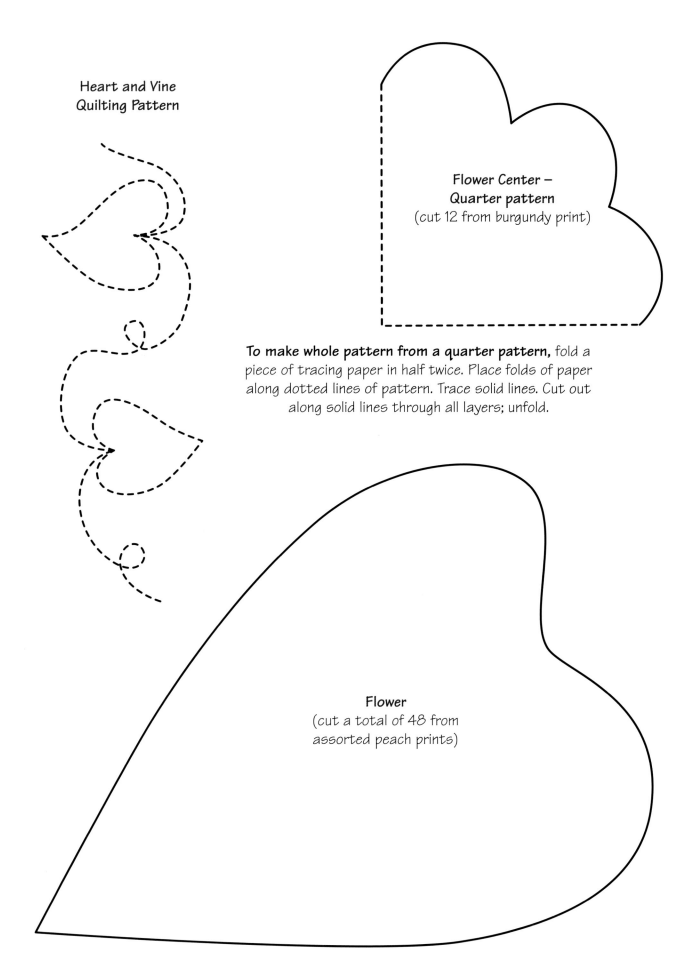

Heart and Vine Quilting Pattern

Flower Center – Quarter pattern
(cut 12 from burgundy print)

To make whole pattern from a quarter pattern, fold a piece of tracing paper in half twice. Place folds of paper along dotted lines of pattern. Trace solid lines. Cut out along solid lines through all layers; unfold.

Flower
(cut a total of 48 from assorted peach prints)

Morning Song

Finished Block Size: $6^{1}/_{2}$" x $16^{1}/_{2}$" (17 cm x 42 cm)
Finished Size: $58^{1}/_{2}$" x $71^{1}/_{2}$" (149 cm x 182 cm)

YARDAGE REQUIREMENTS

Yardage is based on 45" (114 cm) wide fabric. Yardage amounts are based on using the same fabrics for the front and back of your quilt.

Quilt:

$1^{5}/_{8}$ yds (1.49 m) of tan print (appliqué backgrounds)

$1^{7}/_{8}$ yds (1.71 m) of large floral print (block rectangles and outer border)

$1^{1}/_{2}$ yds (1.37 m) of medium floral print (block rectangles and outer border)

$^{5}/_{8}$ yd (57 cm) of small floral print (outer border)

$1^{1}/_{8}$ yds (1.03 m) of tan plaid (block rectangles and outer border)

1 yd (91 cm) of pink print (sashing squares, flowers, outer border)

$1^{1}/_{8}$ yd (1.03 m) of burgundy print (flower centers, bird, inner border)

$3^{1}/_{2}$ yds (3.2 m) of green print (sashing, leaves, outer border, corner squares)

Other fabrics and notions:

1 yd (91 cm) of burgundy print (binding)

$5^{7}/_{8}$ yds (5.37 m) of osnaburg (used in place of batting)

Sulky KK 2000® Temporary Spray Adhesive

Transparent monofilament thread

Before beginning, please read General Instructions, pages 31-35, to familiarize yourself with the techniques used in making this quilt. Use Stitch-and-Clip Method for all seams, unless otherwise noted.

CUTTING

For appliqué backgrounds:

- From tan print, cut 6 strips $8^{1}/_{2}$"w. From osnaburg, cut 3 strips $8^{1}/_{2}$"w.
- Using spray adhesive to secure, layer 1 tan strip (face down), 1 osnaburg strip, and another tan strip (face up). Repeat to make a total of 3 layered strips.
- From layered strips, cut 15 Appliqué Backgrounds $8^{1}/_{2}$" x $7^{1}/_{2}$".

For sashing:

- From green print, cut 26 strips 3"w. From osnaburg, cut 13 strips 3"w.
- Layer strips in same manner as above to make 13 layered strips.
- From layered strips, cut 18 Long Sashings 3" x $17^{1}/_{2}$" and 20 Short Sashings 3" x $7^{1}/_{2}$".

For corner squares:

- From green print, cut 2 strips $5^{1}/_{2}$"w. From osnaburg, cut 1 strip $5^{1}/_{2}$"w.
- Layer strips in same manner as above to make 1 layered strip.
- From layered strip, cut 4 Corner Squares $5^{1}/_{2}$" x $5^{1}/_{2}$".

For sashing squares:

- From pink print, cut 4 strips 3"w. From osnaburg, cut 2 strips 3"w.
- Layer strips in same manner as above to make 2 layered strips.
- From layered strips, cut 24 Sashing Squares 3" x 3".

For inner border:

- From burgundy print, cut 12 strips $2^{1}/_{2}$"w. From osnaburg, cut 6 strips $2^{1}/_{2}$"w.

For block rectangles and outer border:

- Cut the following:
  - large floral print – 12 strips 5"w.
  - medium floral print – 12 strips 4"w.
  - tan plaid – 12 strips 3"w.
  - small floral print – 6 strips 3"w.
  - green print – 6 strips 3"w.
  - pink print – 6 strips 3"w.
  - osnaburg – 6 strips 5"w, 6 strips 4"w, and 15 strips 3"w.
- Layer strips in same manner as above.
- From layered strips, cut the following:
  - large floral print – 15 Block A's 5" x 7½".
  - medium floral print – 15 Block B's 4" x 7½".
  - tan plaid – 15 Block C's 3" x 7½".

Reserve remaining full-length layered strips for outer border.

MAKING APPLIQUÉ BLOCKS

1. Quilt each Appliqué Background using an allover meandering pattern.
2. Use patterns, page 18, to cut out appliqués. Orient Appliqué Backgrounds so that short edges are at top and bottom. Using spray adhesive, arrange appliqués on each Appliqué Background to make 7 Appliqué Block 1's, 7 Appliqué Block 2's, and 1 Appliqué Block 3. Stitch appliqués in place using monofilament thread and a small zigzag stitch to complete each Appliqué Block.

Appliqué Block 1
(make 7)

Appliqué Block 2
(make 7)

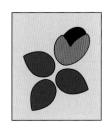

Appliqué Block 3 (make 1)

MAKING THE ROWS

1. For Block Strip 1, refer to diagram below and arrange 1 each of Block A, Block B, Block C, and Appliqué Block 1 (labeled AB-1). Place 2 layered pieces back sides together. Sew along 1 long edge using ½" seam allowance. Clip seam at ½" intervals up to, but not through, the stitching line. Open and lay flat. Using this stitch-and-clip method, sew remaining pieces together to complete Block Strip 1. Repeat to make Block Strips 2-5 as shown.

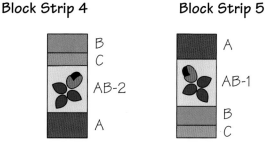

Block Strip 1   **Block Strip 2**   **Block Strip 3**

A, AB-1, B, C

B, AB-2, C, A

C, A, AB-1, B

Block Strip 4   **Block Strip 5**

B, C, AB-2, A

A, AB-1, B, C

2. Sew 6 Long Sashings and Block Strips 1-5 together to make Row 1.

Row 1

3. For Row 2, make 5 Block Strips as shown.

Block Strip 6 **Block Strip 7** **Block Strip 8**

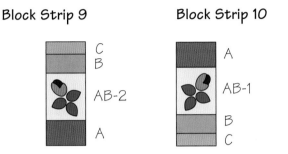

Block Strip 9 **Block Strip 10**

4. Referring to Photo, sew 6 Long Sashings and Block Strips 6-10 together to complete Row 2.

Row 2

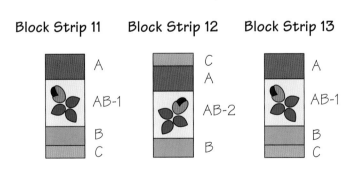

5. For Row 3, make 5 Block Strips as shown.

Block Strip 11 **Block Strip 12** **Block Strip 13**

Block Strip 14 **Block Strip 15**

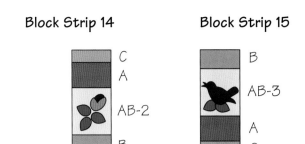

6. Referring to Quilt Diagram, sew 6 Long Sashings and Blocks 11-15 together to complete Row 3.

Row 3

7. Sew 6 Sashing Squares and 5 Short Sashings together to make Sashing Row. Make 4 Sashing Rows.

Sashing Row (make 4)

ASSEMBLING THE QUILT

Refer to photo, page 19, for assembly.

1. Sew Sashing Rows and Rows 1-3 together to complete Quilt Center.

2. For side inner border, match **right sides** and use a ¹/₄" **seam allowance** to sew 6 burgundy print strips together end to end to make 1 long strip; do not clip seam allowances. Repeat for remaining burgundy and matching osnaburg strips. Layer print and osnaburg strips to make 1 long layered strip. From layered strip, cut two 61¹/₂" long Side Inner Borders and two 45¹/₂" long Top/Bottom Inner Borders.

17

3. Sew Top, Bottom, then Side Inner Borders to Quilt Center.
4. For outer border, sew remaining full-length layered strips together as shown to make a Strip Set. Make 3 Strip Sets. Cut across Strip Sets at 5$\frac{1}{2}$" intervals to make 15 Border Sets.

Strip Set (make 3)

Border Sets (make 15)

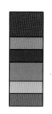

5. Sew Border Sets together to make 1 long strip. From long strip, cut 2 Side Outer Borders 61$\frac{1}{2}$" long and 2 Top/ Bottom Outer Borders 48$\frac{1}{2}$" long.
6. Sew 1 Border Square to each end of each Top/Bottom Outer Border.
7. Sew Side, then Top and Bottom Outer Borders to Inner Border.
8. Follow **Binding**, page 34, to bind quilt.
9. Follow **Washing**, page 35, to wash quilt and fluff seams.

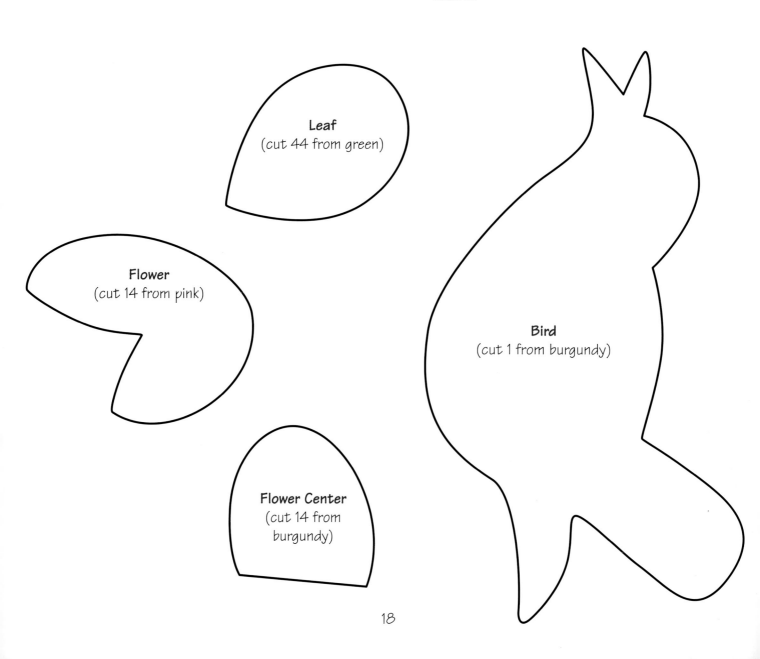

Leaf
(cut 44 from green)

Flower
(cut 14 from pink)

Flower Center
(cut 14 from burgundy)

Bird
(cut 1 from burgundy)

My Beloved Scraps

Finished Block Size: 10" x 10" (25 cm x 25 cm)
Finished Size: 57" x 67" (145 cm x 170 cm)

YARDAGE REQUIREMENTS

Yardage is based on 45" (114 cm) wide fabric. Flannel fabrics work best for this quilt. Make sure to use a coordinating flannel for the backing, since the backing will show in the seams on the front. This quilt does not use a center layer such as fabric or batting.

> 35 fat quarters of assorted flannels (use a good variety of lights, mediums, and darks)
> $1^3/_4$ yds (1.6 m) of red flannel (inner border and binding)
> $4^7/_8$ yds (4.46 m) of solid flannel (backing)

Before beginning, please read General Instructions, pages 31-36, to familiarize yourself with the techniques used in making this quilt. Use Stitch-and-Clip Method for all seams unless otherwise noted.

CUTTING

For square A's, square B's, square C's, and outer border:

- From red and assorted fat quarters, cut 20 Square A's 12" x 12", 20 Square B's 8" x 8", and a total of 78 squares 5" x 5". Use 20 of the 5" x 5" squares for Square C's and remainder for outer border.

For inner border:

- From red flannel, cut 5 strips 5" w.

For backing (use solid flannel for all pieces):

- Cut 7 strips 12"w. From these strips, cut 20 Square A Backings 12" x 12".
- Cut 8 strips 5"w. From these strips, cut 78 Outer Border Backings 5" x 5".
- Cut 5 strips 5"w. Reserve these strips for inner border backing.

MAKING THE BLOCKS

1. Using contrasting colors, layer 1 each of Squares A, B, and C (**Fig. 1**) to make Block. Place a Square A Backing, wrong sides together, under Block. Topstitch $5/_8$" from outer edges of Square B and Square C (**Fig. 2**). Machine quilt Square A, using allover stippling (**Fig. 3**), to complete Large Block. Varying the placement of lights, medium, and darks, repeat step to make a total of 20 Large Blocks.

Fig. 1   Fig. 2   Fig. 3

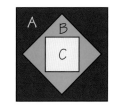 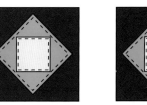

Large Block (make 20)

2. Cut each Large Block in 4 equal parts (**Fig. 4**) to make a total of 80 Small Blocks.

Fig. 4

Small Block (make 80)

3. For 1 Scrap Block, select 4 different Small Blocks. Place 2 of the blocks back sides together. Sew along 1 edge using ½" seam allowance. Clip seam at ½" intervals up to, but not through, the stitching line. Open and lay flat to make Unit 1. Repeat with remaining 2 blocks to make Unit 2. Sew Units together, then clip all seam allowances, to complete Scrap Block. Repeat to make a total of 20 Scrap Blocks.

Unit 1   ### Unit 2

   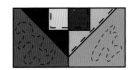

Scrap Block (make 20)

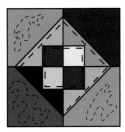

ASSEMBLING THE QUILT

Refer to photo, page 23, for assembly.

1. Sew 4 Scrap Blocks together to make a Row. Make 5 Rows.

Row (make 5)

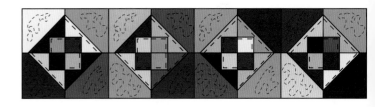

2. Sew Rows together to make Quilt Center.
3. For inner border, match **right sides** and use **¼" seam allowance** to sew 5 inner border strips together end to end to make 1 long strip; do not clip seam allowances. Repeat for inner border backing strips. Layer 1 inner border and 1 backing strip to make 1 long layered strip.
4. Machine quilt layered strip using allover stippling.
5. From layered strip, cut two 51" long Side Inner Border and two 49" long Top/Bottom Inner Border.
6. Sew Side, then Top and Bottom Inner Borders to Quilt Center.
7. For outer border, place each remaining flannel square wrong sides together with a backing square. Quilt a large "X" across each square.
8. Sew 15 outer border squares together; trim to 59" long to make Side Outer Border. Make 2 Side Outer Borders.
9. Sew 14 outer border squares together to make each Top and Bottom Outer Border.
10. Sew Side, then Top and Bottom Outer Borders to Inner Border.
11. Follow **Binding**, page 34, to bind quilt.
12. Follow **Washing**, page 35, to wash and fluff quilt seams.

Sweet Annie

Finished Block Size: 8³/₈" x 12³/₄" (21 cm x 31 cm)
Finished Size: 52" x 65" (132 cm x 165 cm)

YARDAGE REQUIREMENTS

Yardage is based on 45" (114 cm) wide fabric. Yardage amounts are based on using the same fabrics for the front and back of your quilt.

Quilt:

2¹/₈ yds (1.9 m) of cream print (appliqué backgrounds)

2¹/₂ yds (2.3 m) **total** of 10-12 assorted medium prints (sashing)

1 yd (91 cm) of burgundy print (inner border)

3 yds (2.7 m) **total** of 6 assorted green prints (outer border)

Appliqué:

¹/₄ yd (23 cm) **each** of dark pink and dark burgundy print (flowers)

¹/₈ yd (11 cm) **each** of light pink and light burgundy print (flower centers)

¹/₈ yd (11 cm) of blue solid (bows)

¹/₄ yd (23 cm) of dark green print (stems)

¹/₄ yd (23 cm) of green print (leaves)

Other fabrics and notions:

Embroidery floss – cream

9 buttons – ⁵/₈" (16 mm) diameter

1 yd (91 cm) of green print (binding)

4 yds (3.7 m) of osnaburg (used in place of batting)

Sulky KK 2000® Temporary Spray Adhesive

Transparent monofilament thread

Before beginning, please read General Instructions, pages 31-35, to familiarize yourself with the techniques used in making this quilt. Use Stitch-and-Clip Method for all seams, unless otherwise noted.

CUTTING

From cream print:

- Cut 5 strips 13³/₄"w. From these strips, cut 18 Appliqué Backgrounds 13³/₄" x 9³/₈".

From assorted medium prints:

- Cut strips from each print 4"w. From these strips, cut a total of 144 Sashing Rectangles 4" x 5¹/₄". (Cut an even number of rectangles from each print so that you have matching rectangles for top and back of quilt.)

From burgundy print:

- Cut 10 strips 3"w.

From assorted green prints:

- Cut strips from each print 6"w. From these strips, cut a total of 36 Outer Border Rectangles 6" x 14". (It is not critical to cut even numbers of rectangles from each print.)

From osnaburg:

- Cut 3 strips 13³/₄"w. From these strips, cut 9 Appliqué Background fillers 13³/₄" x 9³/₈".
- Cut 9 strips 4"w. From these strips, cut a total of 72 Sashing Rectangle fillers 4" x 5¹/₄".
- Cut 5 strips 3"w for inner border filler.
- Cut 6 strips 6"w for outer border filler.

MAKING APPLIQUÉ BLOCKS

1. Using spray adhesive to secure, layer 1 appliqué background (face down), 1 matching osnaburg filler, and another appliqué background (face up). Machine quilt, using allover stippling and matching thread. Repeat to make 9 appliqué blocks.
2. Use patterns, page 29, to cut out appliqués. Using spray adhesive, arrange appliqués on each appliqué background. Stitch in place using monofilament thread and a small zigzag stitch to complete each Appliqué Block.

Appliqué Block (make 9)

MAKING THE SASHINGS

1. Using spray adhesive to secure, layer 1 Sashing Rectangle (face down), 1 matching osnaburg filler, and another matching Sashing Rectangle (face up). Repeat to make 72 Sashing Rectangles.
2. Place 2 layered Sashing Rectangles back sides together. Sew along 1 short edge using $1/2$" seam allowance. Clip seam at $1/2$" intervals up to, but not through, the stitching line. Open and lay flat. Sew, then clip, another layered Sashing Rectangle to the first two to complete a Short Sashing. Make 12 Short Sashings.

Short Sashing (make 12)

3. Sew 9 Sashing Rectangles together to make Long Sashing. Make 4 Long Sashings.

Long Sashings (make 4)

ASSEMBLING THE QUILT

1. Sew 4 Short Sashings and 3 Appliqué Blocks together to make Row. Make 4 Rows.

Row (make 4)

2. Sew 1 Long Sashing and 1 Row together (sashing will be longer than Row). Trim Long Sashing even with Row. Continue sewing Long Sashings and Rows together to complete Quilt Center.
3. For inner border, match **right sides** and use a $1/4$" seam allowance to sew 5 burgundy strips together end to end to make 1 long strip; do not clip seam allowances. Repeat for remaining burgundy strips and matching filler strips.
4. Layer inner border strips and filler strips to form 1 strip. Quilt strip, using a meandering pattern.
5. Cut inner border strip into two $51 1/4$" long Side Inner Borders and two $42 1/8$" long Top/Bottom Inner Borders. Sew Side, then Top and Bottom Inner Borders to Quilt Center.
6. For outer border, match **right sides** and use a $1/4$" seam allowance to sew Outer Border Rectangles together end to end to make 1 long strip. Cut strip in half. Sew Outer Border filler strips together to make 1 long strip.

7. Layer pieced strips and filler strip. Quilt strip, using a meandering pattern.

8. Cut outer border strip into two 55¼" Side Outer Borders and two 52⅛" Top/Bottom Outer Borders. Sew Side, then Top and Bottom Outer Borders to Inner Borders.

9. Referring to photo, page 25, for placement, use two strands of floss and long stitches to stitch a swirl design in each flower.

10. Sew a button to each bow.

11. Follow **Binding**, page 34, to bind quilt.

12. Follow **Washing**, page 35, to wash quilt to fluff seams.

Quilt Diagram

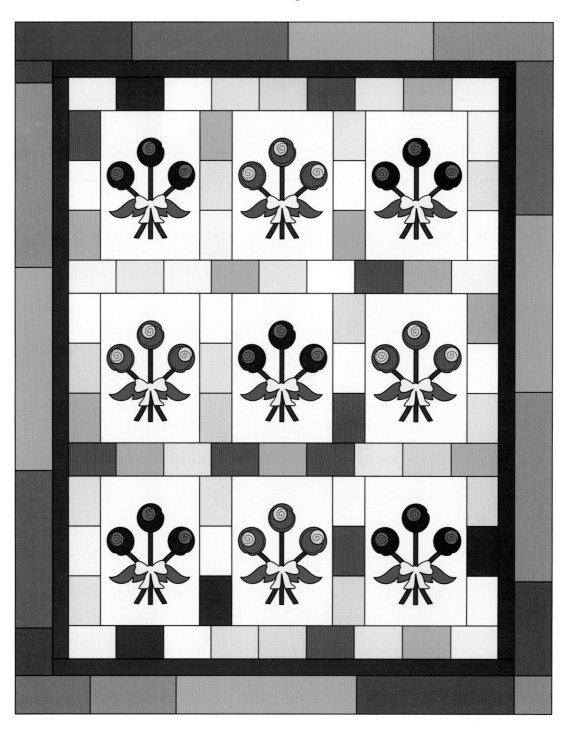

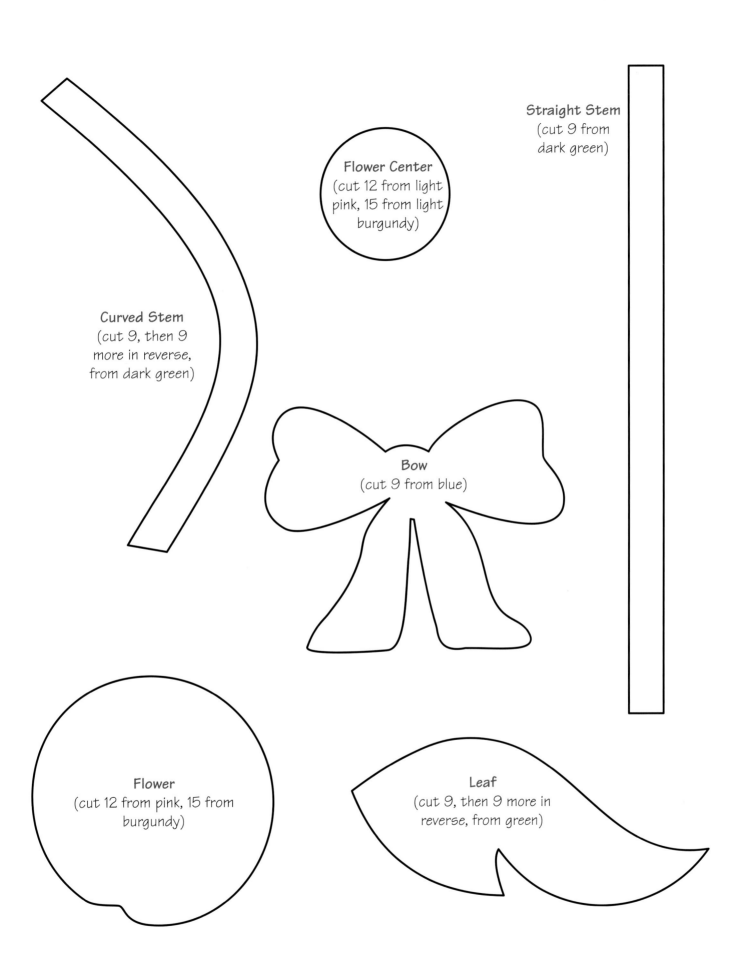

Straight Stem
(cut 9 from
dark green)

Flower Center
(cut 12 from light
pink, 15 from light
burgundy)

Curved Stem
(cut 9, then 9
more in reverse,
from dark green)

Bow
(cut 9 from blue)

Flower
(cut 12 from pink, 15 from
burgundy)

Leaf
(cut 9, then 9 more in
reverse, from green)

Sweet Annie Pillow

Finished Size: 13" x 18" (33 cm x 46 cm)

MATERIALS
Yardage is based on 45" (114 cm) wide fabric.

Scraps of 16 assorted fabrics (blocks)

$^1/_2$ yd (46 cm) of osnaburg (used in place of batting)

1 yd (91 cm) of desired fabric (backing and binding)

Sulky KK 2000® Temporary Spray Adhesive

Polyester fiberfill

Before beginning, please read General Instructions, pages 31-35, to familiarize yourself with the techniques used in making this pillow. Use Stitch-and-Clip Method for all seams, unless otherwise noted.

CUTTING
From *each* scrap:
- Cut 2 Rectangles 4" x 5$^1/_4$".

From osnaburg:
- Cut 2 strips 4"w. From these strips, cut a total of 16 Rectangle fillers 4" x 5$^1/_4$".

From backing fabric:
- Cut two 13" x 9$^1/_2$" pieces for backing.

MAKING PILLOW
1. Using spray adhesive to secure, layer 1 scrap rectangle (face down), 1 matching filler, and 1 matching scrap rectangle (face up). Repeat to make 16 layered Rectangles.
2. Place 2 layered Rectangles back sides together. Sew along 1 short edge using $^1/_2$" seam allowance. Clip seam at $^1/_2$" intervals up to, but not through, the stitching line. Open and lay flat. Sew, then clip, 2 more rectangles to the first two to complete a Row. Make 4 Rows.

Row (make 4)

3. Sew Rows together to complete Pillow Top.

Pillow Top

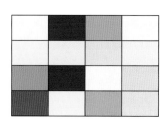

4. For backing, place fabric pieces right sides together. Sew together along 1 short edge; press seam open.
5. Place backing and Pillow Top **wrong sides** together. Baste in place along edges. Follow **Binding**, page 34, to bind edges of pillow.
6. Use a seam ripper to open part of the center seam on pillow back. Stuff pillow with fiberfill. Whipstitch opening closed.
7. Follow **Washing**, page 35, to wash pillow to fluff seams.

General Instructions

To make your project easier and more enjoyable, we encourage you to carefully read all of the general instructions, study the color photographs, and familiarize yourself with the individual project instructions before beginning a project.

SELECTING AND PREPARING FABRICS

Choose high-quality, medium-weight 100% cotton fabrics for the front and back of your quilt. Yardage requirements listed for each project are based on 45" wide fabric with a "usable" width of 42" after shrinkage and trimming selvages. Actual usable widths will vary from fabric to fabric. Our recommended yardage lengths should be adequate for occasional resquaring of fabric when many cuts are required.

It is not necessary to prewash your fabrics when making these projects since you'll wash the finished project to fluff the seams.

A Note About Osnaburg: Most of the quilts in this book use osnaburg fabric as a filler instead of batting. Osnaburg is a more loosely woven variation of muslin that is usually unbleached in color. It makes a great filler for these quilts because the edges fray even more than medium-weight fabrics, creating a fuzzier effect. If osnaburg is unavailable, unbleached muslin may be substituted.

ROTARY CUTTING

For most of the projects it will appear that you are cutting twice the number of pieces (or strips) needed for the front of the quilt. This is correct. Half of the strips will be used for the back of the quilt, half for the front. Matching osnaburg pieces will also be cut for all projects except My Beloved Scraps quilt.

- Place fabric on work surface with fold closest to you.
- Cut all strips from selvage-to-selvage width of fabric unless otherwise indicated in project instructions.
- Square left edge of fabric using rotary cutter and rulers (**Figs. 1 - 2**).

Fig. 1

Fig. 2

- To cut each strip required for a project, place ruler over cut edge of fabric, aligning desired marking on ruler with cut edge; make cut (**Fig. 3**).

Fig. 3

- When cutting several strips from a single piece of fabric, it is important to make sure that cuts remain at a perfect right angle to the fold; square fabric as needed.

LAYERING THE PIECES

Layering the front, filler, and backing pieces together before you ever stitch a seam is the secret to this speedy technique.

Using quilter's spray adhesive eliminates all pinning and keeps your quilt layers from shifting when quilting and piecing. If necessary, you may substitute pinning instead of using the spray.

1. To prepare pieces, lay matching quilt front and back pieces (or strips) wrong side up on a flat, covered surface. Spray the spray adhesive on the wrong sides of the fabrics.
2. Place back piece (wrong side up) on a clean surface. Aligning edges, place a matching osnaburg filler piece on top. To adhere, use your fingers to lightly press the fabrics together.
3. Aligning edges, place the top piece (right side up) on the osnaburg, then press in place with fingers to complete the layered piece.

MACHINE APPLIQUÉING

Projects in this book use two types of machine appliqué: a Blanket Stitch appliqué and invisible appliqué that uses monofilament thread. Choose whichever method you like.

1. Pin stabilizer, such as lightweight paper or any of the commercially available products, on wrong side of background fabric before stitching appliqués in place.
2. Set up sewing machine with desired type of thread in the needle and a general-purpose sewing thread that matches the background fabric in the bobbin.
3. For Blanket stitch appliqué, refer to your machine's owner's manual to set up machine. For invisible appliqué, set sewing machine for a small (scant $1/8$") zigzag stitch and a medium stitch length.
4. Begin by stitching 2 or 3 stitches in place (drop feed dogs or set stitch length at 0) to anchor thread. Stitch over all exposed raw edges of appliqué pieces, following Steps 5-8 below for corners and curves.

5. (**Note:** Dots on **Figs. 4 – 9** indicate where to leave needle in fabric when pivoting.) For outside corners, stitch just past corner, stopping with needle in background fabric (**Fig. 4**). Raise presser foot. Pivot project, lower presser foot, and stitch adjacent side (**Fig. 5**).

Fig. 4   **Fig. 5**

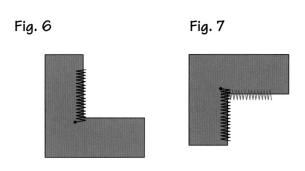

6. For inside corners, stitch just past corner, stopping with needle in appliqué fabric (**Fig. 6**). Raise presser foot. Pivot project, lower presser foot, and stitch adjacent side (**Fig. 7**).

Fig. 6   **Fig. 7**

7. When stitching outside curves, stop with needle in background fabric. Raise presser foot and pivot project as needed. Lower presser foot and continue stitching, pivoting as often as necessary to follow curve (**Fig. 8**).

Fig. 8

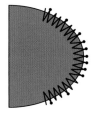

8. When stitching inside curves, stop with needle in appliqué fabric. Raise presser foot and pivot project as needed. Lower presser foot and continue stitching, pivoting as often as necessary to follow curve (**Fig. 9**).

Fig. 9

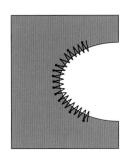

9. Do not backstitch at end of stitching. Pull threads to wrong side of background fabric; knot thread and trim ends.

10. Carefully tear away stabilizer.

QUILTING

Unlike traditional quilting, the quilting on these quilts usually takes place before you begin piecing!

All the quilt projects are machine quilted using free-motion quilting. If you are not already a free-motion quilter, these quilts are good ones to practice on, since quilting is done on individual pieces rather than on an entire, bulky quilt.

Free-Motion Quilting

Most of the quilting is done in random curved lines and swirls called "meandering" quilting. Quilting lines should not cross or touch each other. This type of quilting does not need to be marked. If you choose to use a quilting pattern, use your favorite water-removable marking tool to transfer lines to pieces.

1. Thread sewing machine with a general-purpose sewing thread that matches front and back fabrics of the layered piece.

2. Attach darning foot to sewing machine and lower or cover feed dogs.

3. Position layered piece under darning foot. Holding top thread, take 1 stitch and pull bobbin thread to top of piece. To "lock" beginning of quilting line, hold top and bobbin threads while making 3 to 5 stitches in place.

4. Use 1 hand on each side of darning foot to move fabric through the machine. Even stitch length is achieved by using smooth, flowing hand motion and steady machine speed. Slow machine speed and fast hand movement will create long stitches. Fast machine speed and slow hand movement will create short stitches. Move quilt sideways, back and forth, in a circular motion, or in a random motion to create desired designs; do not rotate quilt. Lock stitches at end of each quilting line.

PIECING

The assembly method used on these projects is extremely forgiving, because the fluffed seams will cover up intersections where different pieces meet. Matching corners exactly is not critical.

NOTE: All seams use a $^1/_2$" seam allowance. If you do a lot of traditional piecing, this will not feel normal at all. Do not hesitate to add a line of tape to your sewing machine throat plate until you get accustomed to the wider seam allowance.

Stitch-and-Clip Method

1. Place 2 layered pieces **back sides** together.

2. Use a $^1/_2$" **seam allowance** to stitch pieces together. The seam allowance will be on the **front** of the quilt.

3. Before you open up the pieces, use sharp embroidery scissors to make straight clips into the seam allowance at $^3/_8$"-$^1/_2$" intervals up to, but not through, the stitching line.

4. Open up the pieces and lay flat. Press the clipped seam allowance to 1 side.

5. Proceed to the next seam, making sure to clip each seam allowance after stitching.

MAKING A HANGING SLEEVE

Attaching a hanging sleeve to back of wall hanging or quilt before the binding is added allows your project to be displayed on a wall.

1. Measure width of quilt top edge and subtract 1". Cut piece of fabric 7"w by determined measurement.

2. Press short edges of fabric piece ¼" to wrong side; press edges ¼" to wrong side again and machine stitch in place.

3. Matching wrong sides, fold piece in half lengthwise to form tube.

4. Matching raw edges, center hanging sleeve along top edge on back of quilt. Baste top edge in place. (When binding is added, treat hanging sleeve as part of quilt back.)

5. Blindstitch bottom of hanging sleeve to backing, taking care not to stitch through to front of quilt.

BINDING

Cut width of binding fabric allows for using a ¹/₂" seam allowance when stitching.

Making Binding

1. To determine length of strip needed if attaching binding with mitered corners, measure edges of quilt and add 6"-12".

2. Cut strips of binding fabric 2¹/₂" wide or the width specified in the project instructions. Piece strips to achieve necessary length.

3. Matching wrong sides and long edges, press strip in half lengthwise to complete binding.

Attaching Binding

1. Beginning with 1 end near center on bottom edge of quilt on right side of quilt, match raw edge of binding to raw edge of quilt top. Pin binding to right side of quilt along 1 edge.

2. When you reach first corner, mark ¹/₂" from corner of quilt top (**Fig. 10**).

Fig. 10

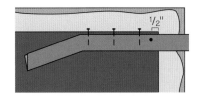

3. Beginning 10" from end of binding and using ¹/₂" seam allowance, sew binding to quilt, backstitching at beginning of stitching and at mark (**Fig. 11**). Lift needle out of fabric and clip thread.

Fig. 11

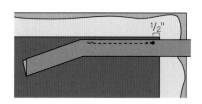

4. Fold binding as shown in **Figs. 12 – 13** and pin binding to adjacent side, matching raw edges. When reaching the next corner, mark ¹/₂" from edge of quilt top.

Fig. 12   **Fig. 13**

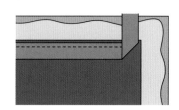 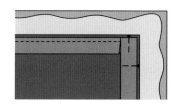

5. Backstitching at edge of quilt top, sew pinned binding to quilt (**Fig. 14**); backstitch at the next mark. Lift needle out of fabric and clip thread.

Fig. 14

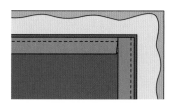

6. Repeat Steps 4 and 5 to continue sewing binding to quilt, leaving 10" of binding unsewn at end (**Fig. 15**).

Fig. 15

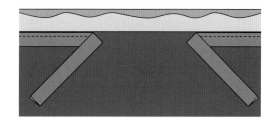

7. Bring beginning and end of binding to center of opening and fold each end back, leaving a 1/4" space between folds (**Fig. 16**). Finger-press folds.

Fig. 16

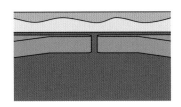

8. Unfold ends of binding and draw a line across wrong side in finger-pressed crease. Draw a line through the lengthwise pressed fold of binding at same spot to create a cross mark. With edge of ruler at marked cross, line up 45° angle marking on ruler with one long side of binding. Draw a diagonal line from edge to edge. Repeat on remaining end, making sure that the two lines are angled the same way (**Fig. 17**).

Fig. 17

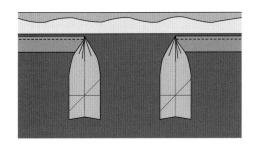

9. Matching right sides and diagonal lines, pin binding ends together at right angles (**Fig. 18**).

Fig. 18

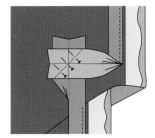

10. Machine stitch along diagonal line, removing pins as you stitch (**Fig. 19**).

Fig. 19

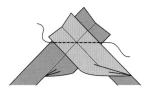

11. Lay binding against quilt to double-check that it is correct length.
12. Trim binding ends, leaving 1/4" seam allowance; press seam open. Stitch binding to quilt.
13. If using 2 1/2"w binding (finished size 1/2"), trim backing and batting a scant 1/2" larger than quilt top so that batting and backing will fill the binding when it is folded over to quilt backing.
14. On 1 edge of quilt, fold binding over to quilt backing and pin pressed edge in place, covering stitching line (**Fig. 20**). On adjacent side, fold binding over, forming a mitered corner (**Fig. 21**). Repeat to pin remainder of binding in place.

Fig. 20   **Fig. 21**

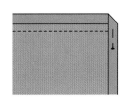   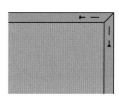

15. Blindstitch binding to backing, taking care not to stitch through to front of quilt.

WASHING

The final step for completing your quilt is giving it a good wash to fluff and scruff up the clipped seams, which makes them look just like chenille.

1. Wash quilt in the washing machine using gentle cycle and cold water. Use a small amount of gentle detergent in the water.
2. Place quilt in the dryer with several clean tennis balls or small tennis shoes. Dry quilt using the delicate or low heat setting.

Metric Conversion Chart

Inches x 2.54 = centimeters (cm)
Inches x 25.4 = millimeters (mm)
Inches x .0254 = meters (m)

Yards x .9144 = meters (m)
Yards x 91.44 = centimeters (cm)
Centimeters x .3937 = inches (")
Meters x 1.0936 = yards (yd)

Standard Equivalents

⅛"	3.2 mm	0.32 cm	⅛ yard	11.43 cm	0.11 m
¼"	6.35 mm	0.635 cm	¼ yard	22.86 cm	0.23 m
⅜"	9.5 mm	0.95 cm	⅜ yard	34.29 cm	0.34 m
½"	12.7 mm	1.27 cm	½ yard	45.72 cm	0.46 m
⅝"	15.9 mm	1.59 cm	⅝ yard	57.15 cm	0.57 m
¾"	19.1 mm	1.91 cm	¾ yard	68.58 cm	0.69 m
⅞"	22.2 mm	2.22 cm	⅞ yard	80 cm	0.8 m
1"	25.4 mm	2.54 cm	1 yard	91.44 cm	0.91 m

Production Team: Technical Writers — Jean Lewis and Sherry O'Connor; Production Artist — Amy Gerke; Photo Stylist — Janna Laughlin.